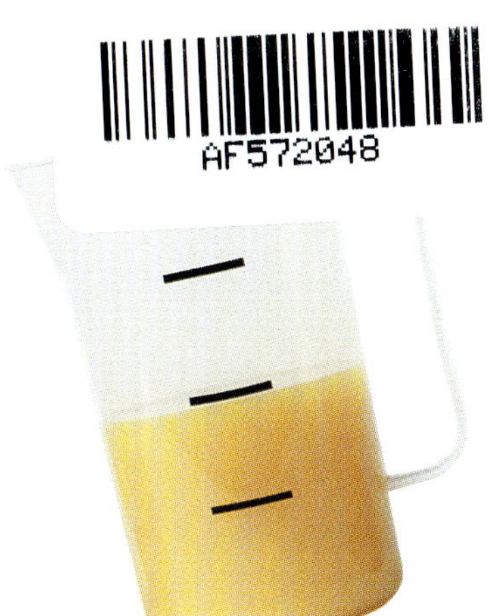

Dictionary of **Mathematical Terms**

By Catherine A. Welch

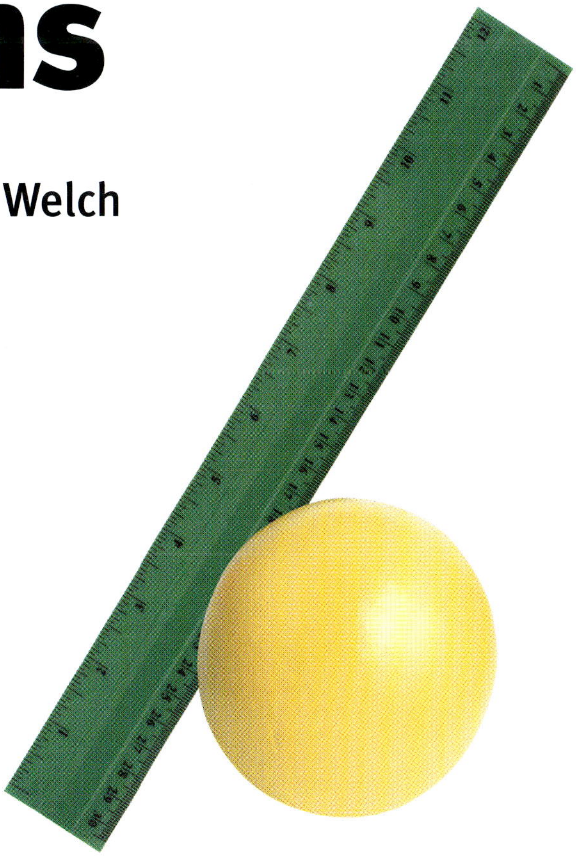

CELEBRATION PRESS
Pearson Learning Group

Contents

Math is used everywhere—in building, sports, music, cooking, and other areas.

Why Use the Dictionary?

When you study mathematics, numbers are important—but so are words. To understand math ideas, you must learn the language of mathematics. This dictionary will help you understand the meaning of many special math words or terms.

You'll find these words when you learn math in school. They will help you to ask questions about math problems. You will use these words to discuss and write solutions to math problems. Math can be fun if you know the language of mathematics.

How to Use This Dictionary

In this dictionary, the math words appear in boldfaced type. These boldfaced words are called entry words. Next to each entry word is its definition.

You will also find two guide words at the top of each page. These words are the first and last entry words on the page. The entry words between the guide words are listed in alphabetical order.

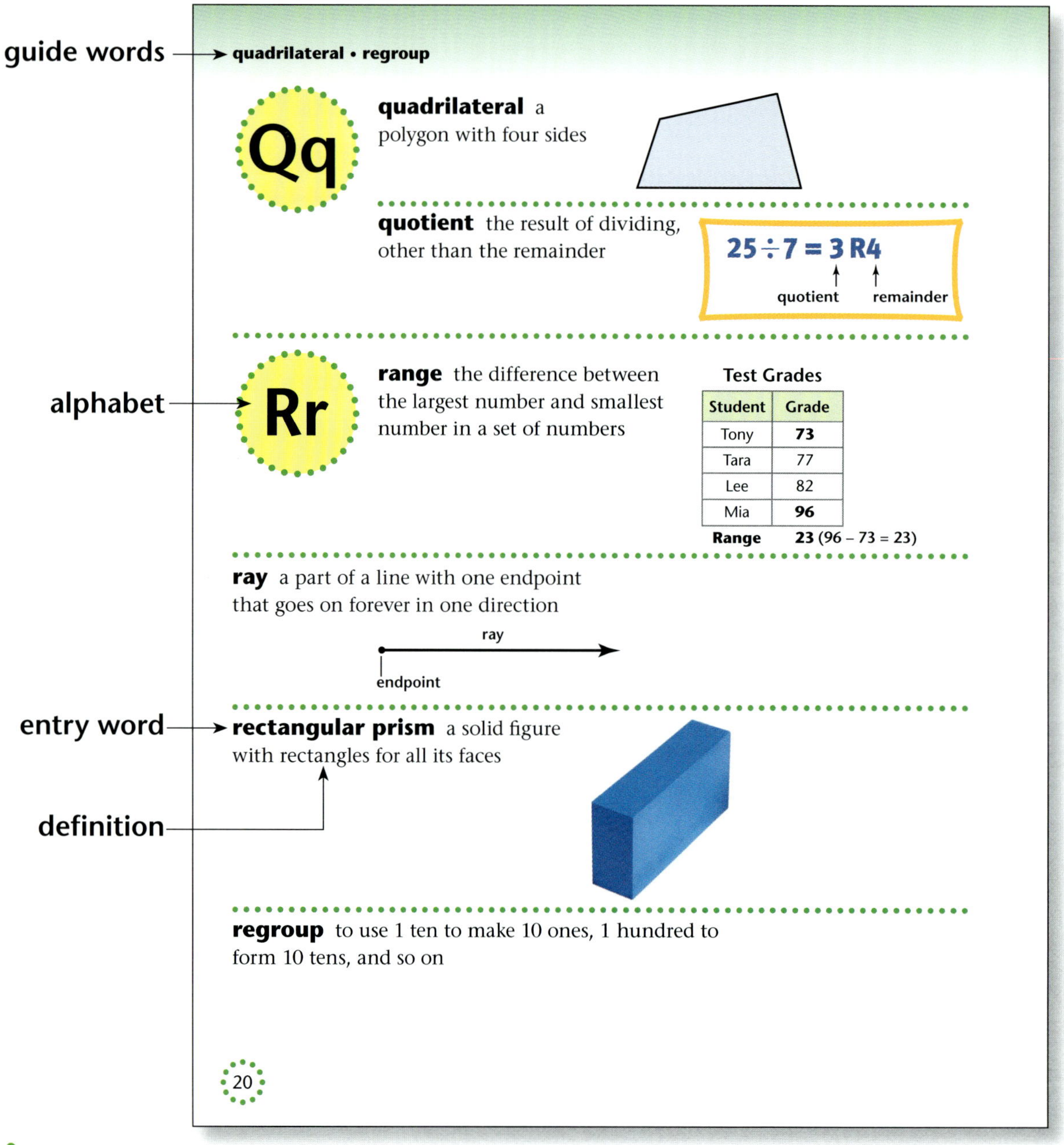

quadrilateral • regroup

Qq

quadrilateral a polygon with four sides

quotient the result of dividing, other than the remainder

$25 \div 7 = 3\ R4$

quotient remainder

Rr

range the difference between the largest number and smallest number in a set of numbers

Test Grades

Student	Grade
Tony	**73**
Tara	77
Lee	82
Mia	**96**
Range	**23** (96 – 73 = 23)

ray a part of a line with one endpoint that goes on forever in one direction

ray
endpoint

rectangular prism a solid figure with rectangles for all its faces

regroup to use 1 ten to make 10 ones, 1 hundred to form 10 tens, and so on

20

acute angle an angle less than a right angle; an angle less than 90° (*See also* **angle**; **right angle**.)

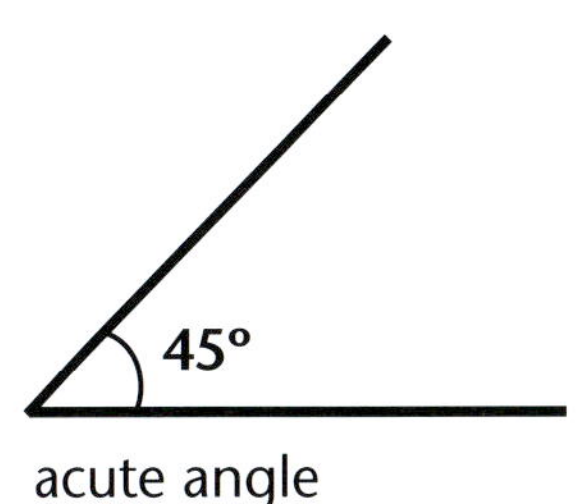

acute angle

acute triangle a triangle with three acute angles (*See also* **acute angle**.)

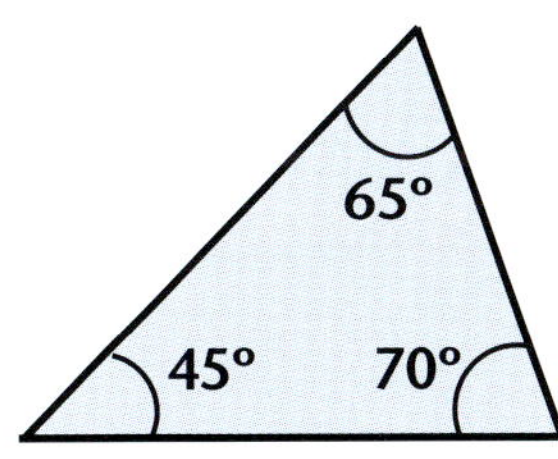

Each angle is less than 90°.

angle what is formed when two lines or rays meet; an angle is measured in degrees (*See also* **ray**.)

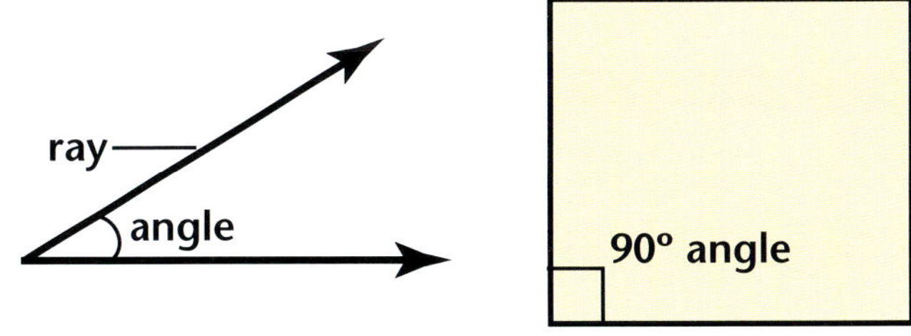

area the amount of space inside a flat figure; to find the area of a rectangle, multiply the length times width, or $A = l \times w$

This boy finds the area of this rectangular grass patch by multiplying the length by the width.

average the mean of a group of numbers; add all numbers in a group, and then divide by the number of numbers in that group (*See also* **mean**.)

Find the average: 4, 16, 8, 12

$$4 + 16 + 8 + 12 = 40$$

$$40 \div 4 = 10$$

The average of the 4 numbers is 10.

bar graph a graph that uses bars to show and compare data (*See also* **data**.)

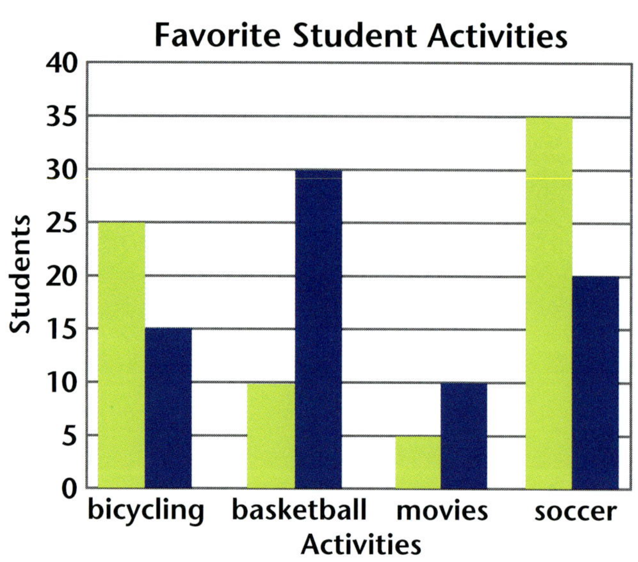

A double bar graph can be used to compare two sets of data.

benchmark fractions fractions that can be used to compare other fractions (*See also* **estimate**, **fraction**.)

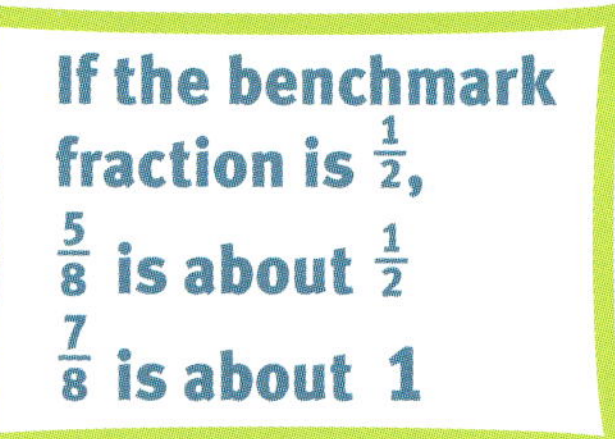

capacity the amount a container or space can hold when completely filled

This pitcher is filled to capacity.

centimeter (cm) a metric unit of length; 100 centimeters equals 1 meter (*See also* **meter**; **metric system**.)

1 centimeter equals about 0.4 inches

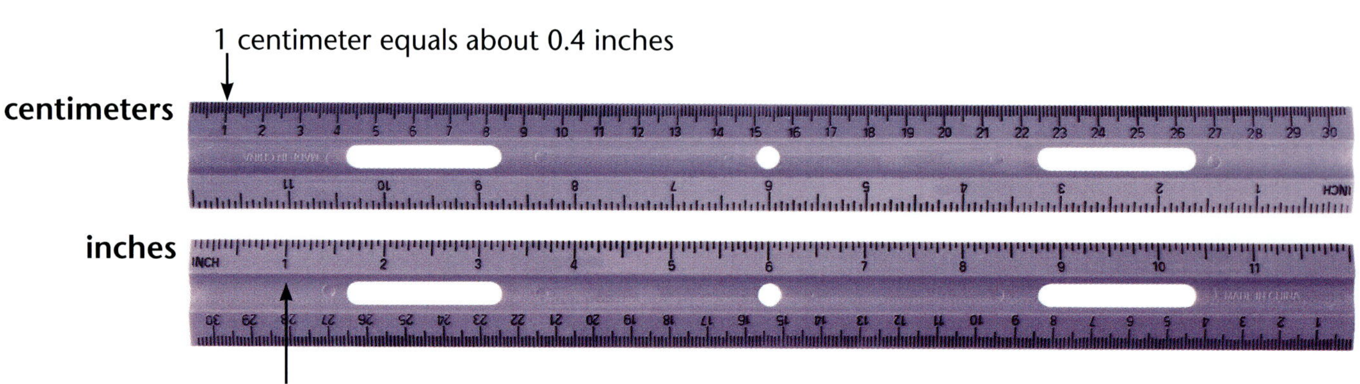

1 inch equals about 2.5 centimeters

circle a closed plane figure in which all points on the edge are the same distance from the center point (*See also* **plane figure**.)

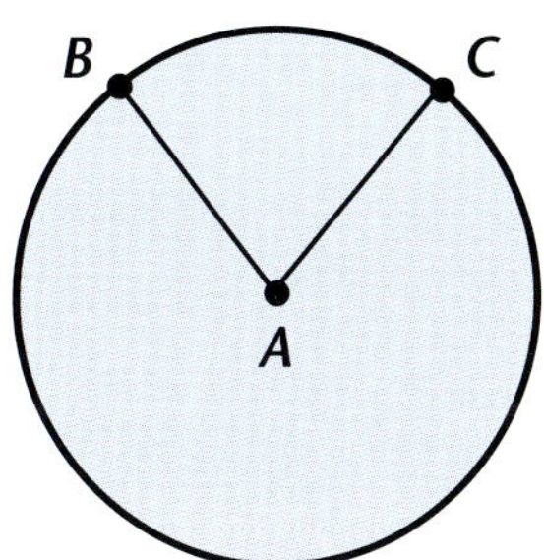

The distance from *A* (the center point) to *B* is the same as the distance from *A* to *C*.

circle graph (also called a pie chart) the whole circle stands for 100% and is divided into parts; the graph shows each part's share of 100%

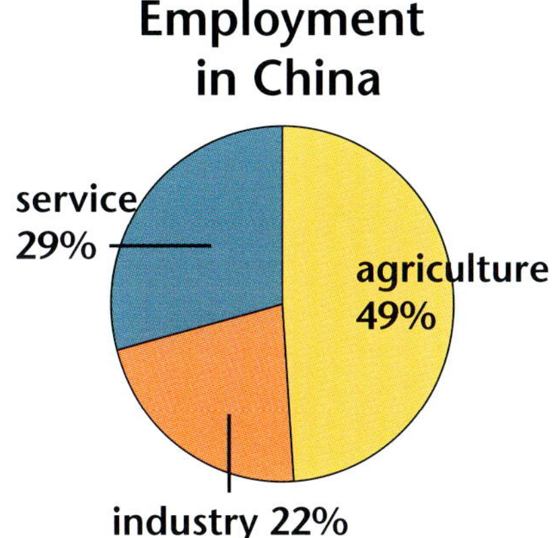

This circle graph shows the percentage of people in China who work in three major areas.

Commutative Property the order in which addends or factors are added or multiplied does not change the sum or the product (*See also* **factors**, **sum**.)

5 x 3 = 15

3 x 5 = 15

composite number a whole number that is divisible by 1, itself, and at least one other whole number (*See also* **divisible**, **factors**.)

6, 15, and 32 are composite numbers;
6 is divisible by 1, 2, and 3

cone a solid figure that has one circular flat surface and one curved surface that meet in a point (*See also* **solid figure**.)

congruent figures two or more figures that have the same size and shape

These two solid figures are congruent.

coordinate grid a grid of intersecting lines used to show ordered pairs. (*See also* **ordered pair**.)

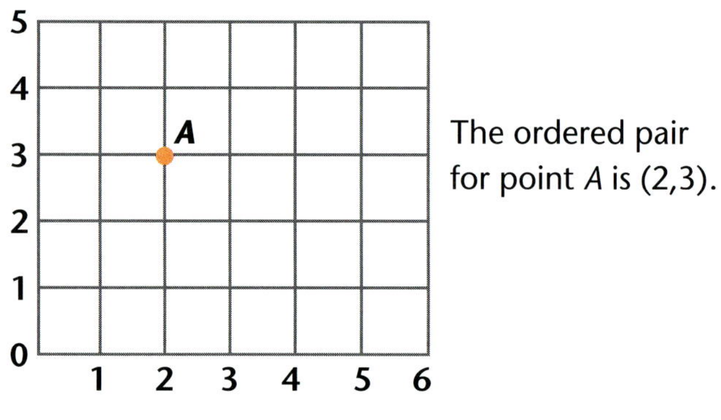

The ordered pair for point *A* is (2,3).

customary units of measure system used in the United States to measure length, capacity, and weight (*See also* **capacity**.)

Length	1 foot (ft) = 12 inches (in.)
	1 yard (yd) = 36 inches (in.); 3 feet (ft)
	1 mile = 5,280 feet (ft); 1,760 yards (yd)
Area	1 square foot (ft^2) = 144 square inches (in^2)
Volume	1 cubic foot (ft^3) = 1,728 cubic inches (in^3)
Capacity	1 tablespoon (tbsp) = 3 teaspoons (tsp)
	1 fluid ounce (fl oz) = 2 tablespoons (tbsp)
	1 cup (c) = 8 fluid ounces (fl oz)
	1 pint (pt) = 2 cups (c)
	1 quart (qt) = 2 pints (pt)
	1 gallon (gal) = 4 quarts (qt)
Weight	1 pound (lb) = 16 ounces (oz)
	1 ton (T) = 2,000 pounds (lb)

This chart shows examples of customary units of measure.

cylinder a solid figure that has a curved surface and two congruent circular faces

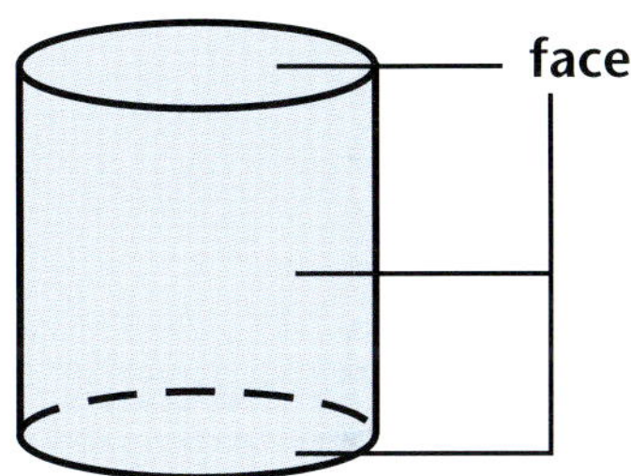

A silo that holds grain is a cylinder.

data information gathered to make calculations

decimal a number with one or more places to the right of the decimal point

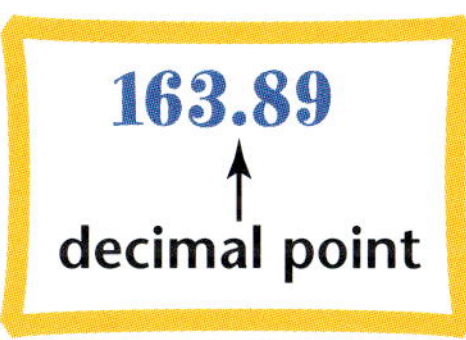

decimeter (dm) a metric unit of length; 10 decimeters equal 1 meter (*See also* **centimeter**, **meter**, **metric system**.)

degrees Celsius (°C) a unit of temperature used by scientists and in many countries (*See also* **degrees Fahrenheit**.)

On the Celsius scale, 0° is the freezing point of water, and 100° is the boiling point of water. On the Fahrenheit scale, 32° is the freezing point of water, and 212° is the boiling point of water.

degrees Fahrenheit (°F) a unit of temperature used in the United States (*See also* **degrees Celsius**.)

denominator the number below the fraction bar in a fraction (*See also* **fraction**.)

For the fraction $\frac{4}{7}$,
the denominator is 7.

diagonal a line segment other than a side that connects two vertices of a polygon (*See also* **vertex**.)

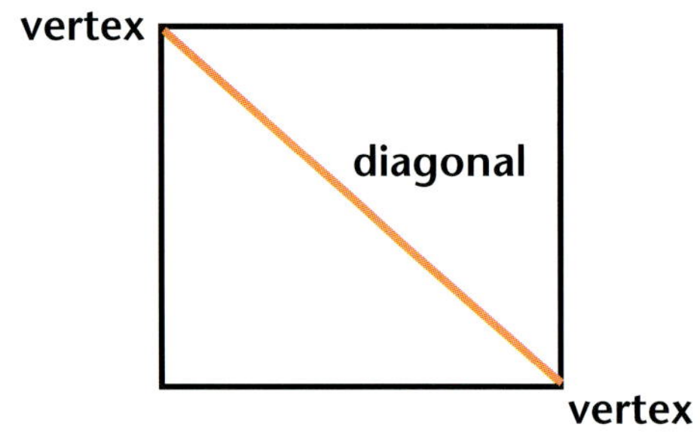

difference the number that is the result of subtraction

$14 - 6 = 8$
The difference is 8.

dividend the number to be divided in a division operation

$4\overline{)16}$ or $16 \div 4$
The dividend is 16.

divisible able to be divided with no remainder (*See also* **quotient**.)

$8 \div 2 = 4$ or $2\overline{)8}$ (quotient 4)
The quotient is 4, with no remainder.

divisor the number by which another number is divided (*See also* **dividend**.)

$21 \div 3 = 7$

The divisor is 3.

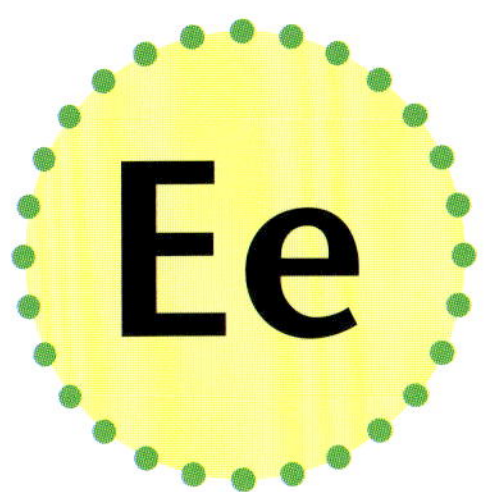

edge a line segment where two faces of a solid meet (*See also* **face**.)

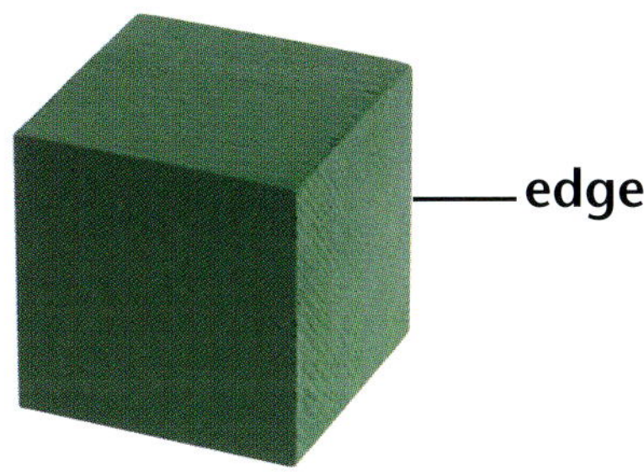

equation a mathematical statement that two expressions are equal; an equation may include variables (*See also* **variable**.)

$8 \times 4 = 32$

$a + 4 = 6 + y$

equilateral triangle a triangle with three equal angles and three sides the same length

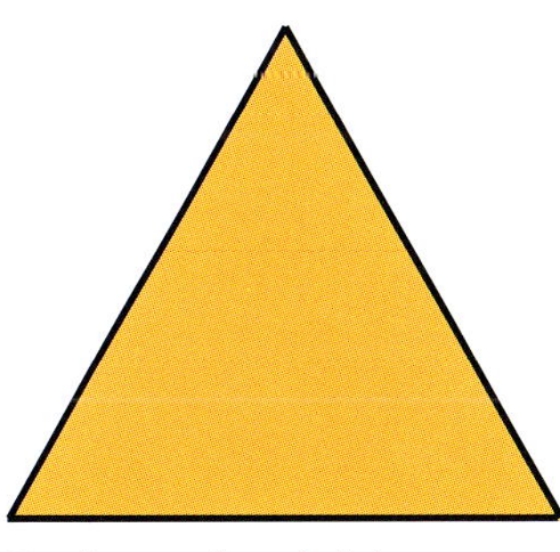

Each angle of this equilateral triangle is 60°.

equivalent fractions fractions that have the same value

$\frac{1}{2} = \frac{2}{4} = \frac{4}{8}$

estimate an approximate rather than exact answer; to give an approximate answer

face the outside flat surface of a solid figure

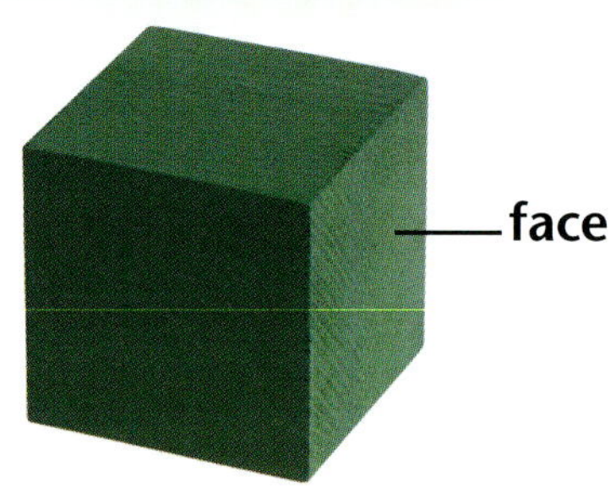

factors numbers multiplied together to give a product.

5 x 3 = 15
5 and 3 are factors.
15 is the product.

fluid ounce (fl oz) a customary unit used to measure capacity (*See also* **capacity**.)

This cup is filled with 8 fluid ounces of liquid.

fraction a number used to show a part of a whole

$\frac{1}{8}$ $\frac{2}{3}$ $\frac{4}{5}$

One of the 16 smaller squares sits apart from the main large square. This smaller square is $\frac{1}{16}$ of the whole.

gram (g) a metric unit of mass; 25 grams is about 1 ounce (*See also* **mass**, **metric system**.)

These pennies weigh about 37 grams.

hundredth one part of a whole that contains 100 equal parts

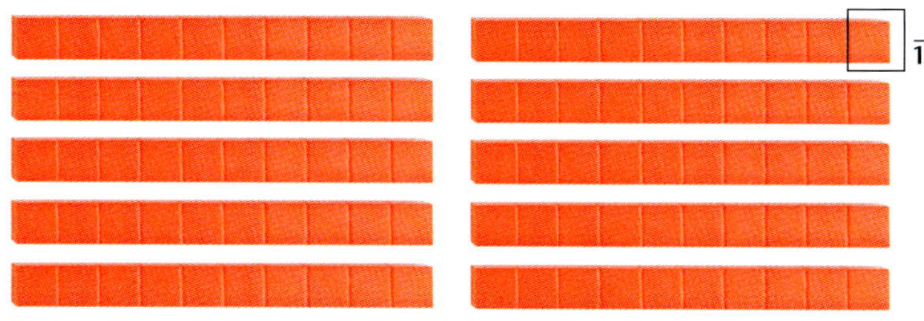

This snap cube is one hundredth of the total number of cubes shown.

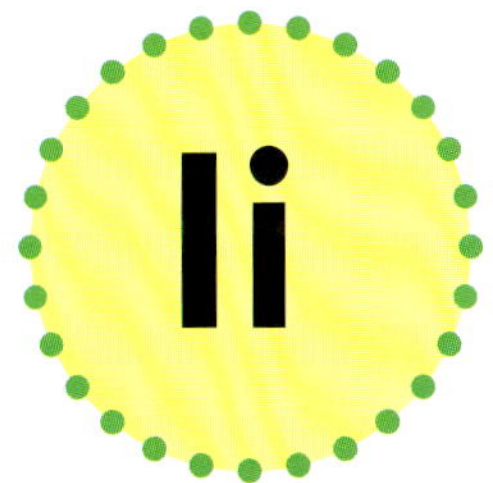

improper fraction a fraction with a numerator greater than or equal to its denominator (*See also* **denominator**, **fraction**, **numerator**.)

$\frac{6}{3}$ $\frac{7}{2}$ $\frac{5}{5}$

intersecting lines lines that cross each other at one point

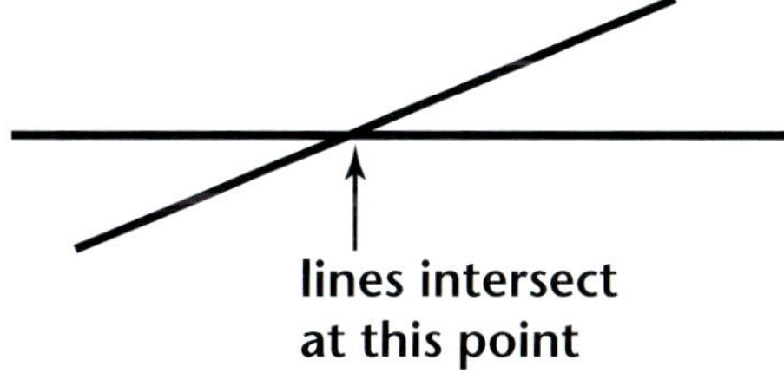

interval a set of numbers between two endpoints; a closed interval includes the endpoint, while an open interval does not

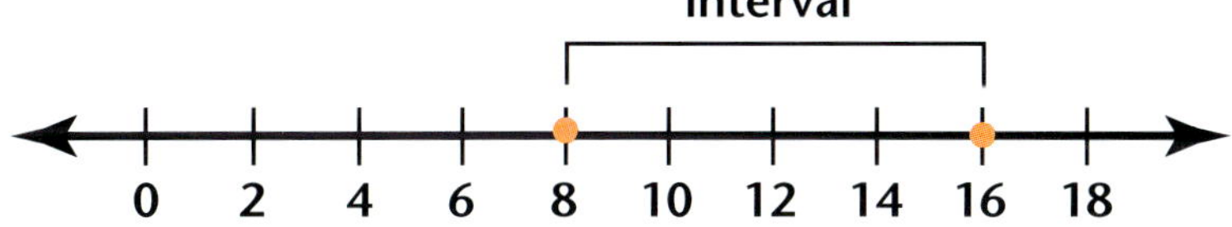

This closed interval includes all the numbers between 8 and 16, including 8 and 16.

isosceles triangle a triangle with two equal sides and two equal angles

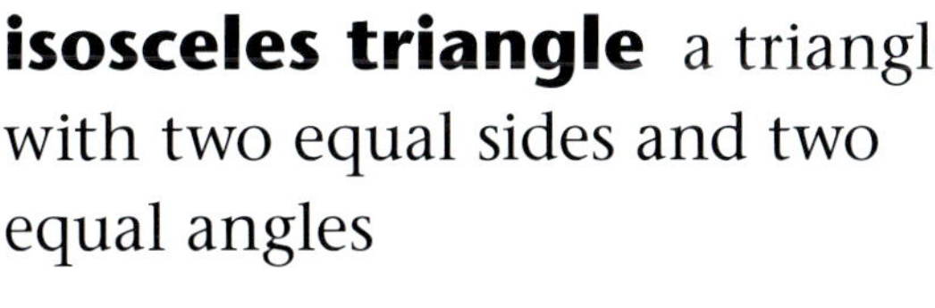

100°
40°
40°

In this isosceles triangle, two angles are 40°. The sides opposite these angles are equal in length.

kilogram (kg) a metric unit of mass; 1 kilogram is about 2.2 pounds (*See also* **metric system**.)

kilometer (km) a metric unit of length; 1 kilometer is about 0.6 mile; 1 kilometer equals 1,000 meters (*See also* **metric system**.)

This pool is 50 meters long. One lap equals 100 meters. The swimmer must do 10 laps to swim 1 kilometer.

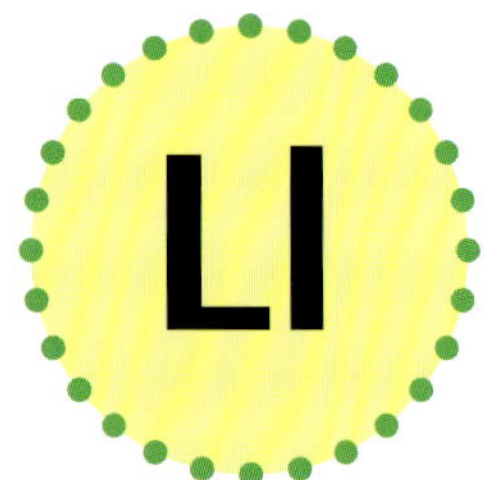

line a straight path of points with no thickness and no endpoints (*See also* **line segment**.)

This line goes on forever in each direction.

line graph a graph that changes information into points on a grid, which can show changes in information over a period of time

India's Population Growth

Population in Millions: 1,100,000; 1,050,000; 1,000,000; 950,000

Year: 1999, 2001, 2003, 2005

line plot a graph that shows information on a number line

This line plot shows the number of books read during summer vacation: *x* stands for one student; 6 students read 3 books.

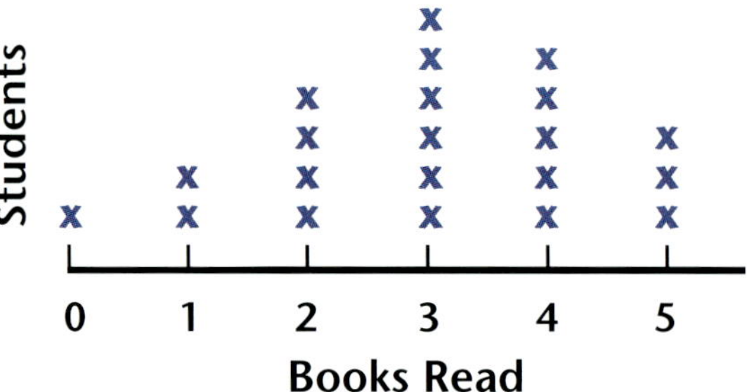

line segment a part of a line with endpoints; the shortest distance between two points (*See also* **line**.)

A •———————• *B*

A and *B* are the endpoints of this line segment.

liter (L) a metric unit of capacity; 1 liter is about 2.1 pints (*See also* **capacity**, **metric system**.)

This bottle contains 1 liter of juice. A liter is slightly more than a quart.

mass the amount of matter in an object (*See also* **gram**.)

These stones have a greater mass than the feathers.

mathematical symbols symbols that show a mathematical operation or information

+ add	$<$ less than
− subtract	$>$ greater than
× multiply	$\geq$ greater than or equal to
÷ divide	= equals

mean the average of a group of numbers (*See also* **average**.)

median the middle number in an ordered set of numbers; with an even number of numbers, the median is the average of the two middle numbers (*See also* **average**.)

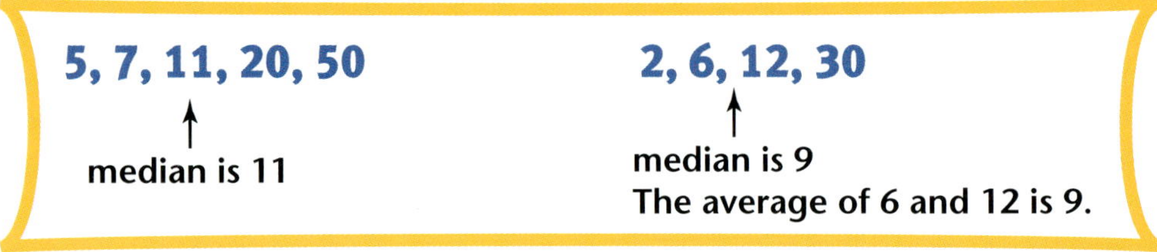

meter (m) a metric unit of length; a meter is a little more than a yard (*See also* **metric system**.)

This baseball bat is about a meter long.

metric system a system of measurement using the meter, kilogram, and liter (*See also* **kilogram**, **liter**, **meter**.)

millennium a period of 1,000 years

The year 2000 was the end of the second millennium.

milliliter (ml) a metric unit of capacity; 1,000 milliliters equals 1 liter (*See also* **liter**.)

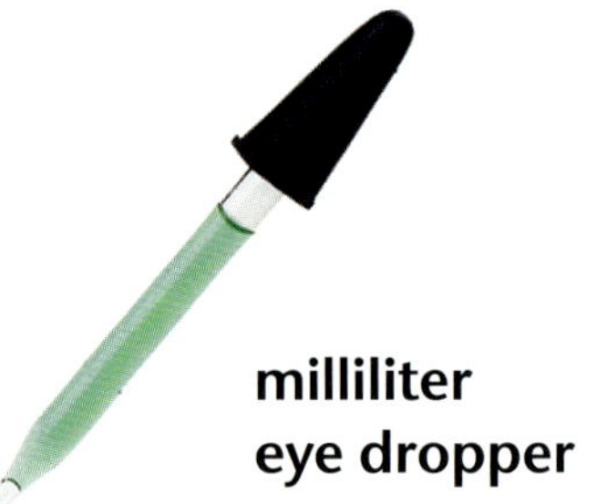

milliliter eye dropper

millimeter (mm) a metric unit of length; 1,000 millimeters equals 1 meter (*See also* **meter**.)

A ladybug is anywhere between 3 and 10 millimeters long.

mode the number or numbers that occur most often in a set of information

Number of Students in Each Sport

	Baseball	Basketball	Ice Hockey	Soccer
Grade 4	22	16	3	12
Grade 5	25	14	3	18
Grade 6	30	16	5	21
Mode		**16**	**3**	

Some sets have no mode.

multiple the product of any two whole numbers

number sentence a horizontal mathematical expression that contains at least two numbers and at least one operation

$16 \div 4$ or $2(3 + 6)$

numerator the number above the fraction bar in a fraction

$\frac{7}{3}$ ← numerator

obtuse angle an angle more than 90° but less than 180°

120°

obtuse triangle a triangle that has one obtuse angle (*See also* **obtuse angle**.)

This triangle has one angle greater than 90°.

120°

ordered pair a pair of numbers that show the location of a point on a coordinate grid (*See also* **coordinate grid**.)

parallel lines lines that never meet and are always the same distance apart (*See also* **line**.)

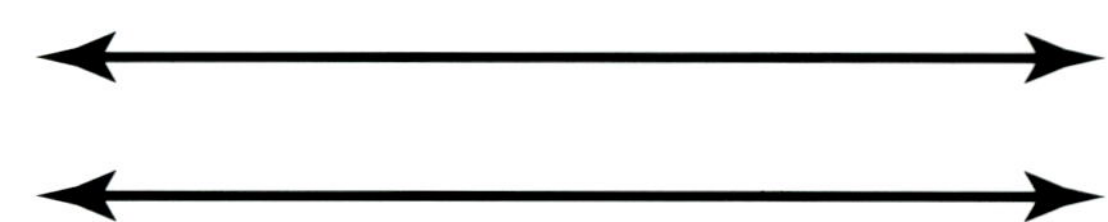

parallelogram a 4-sided polygon with two pairs of opposite parallel sides

perimeter distance around the outside of a plane figure; to find the perimeter of a rectangle, add all four sides, or $P = l + l + w + w$

Measure the length of each side to find the perimeter.

perpendicular lines lines that cross each other at a right angle (*See also* **right angle**.)

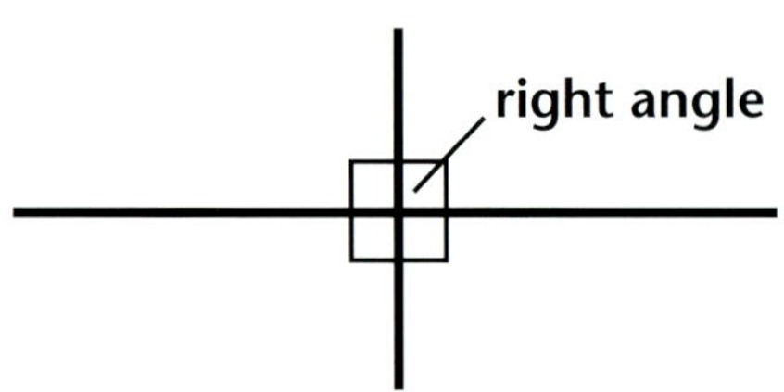

Each angle is 90°.

place value the value of a digit depending on its position in a number

place values of the number 1,357

plane figure a geometric figure with all points lying on one plane, such as square, circle, triangle

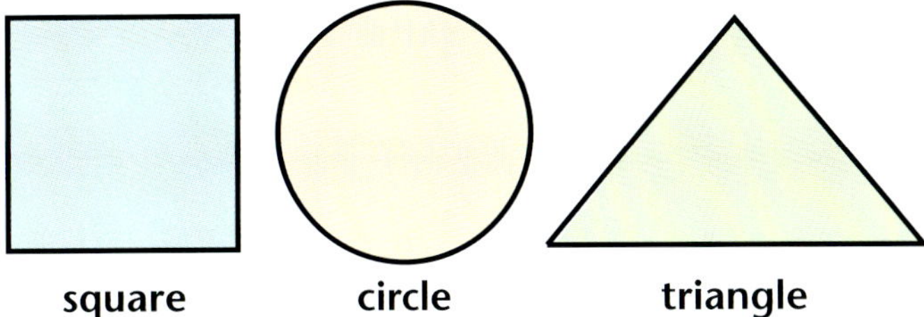

polygon a closed plane figure with three or more line segments

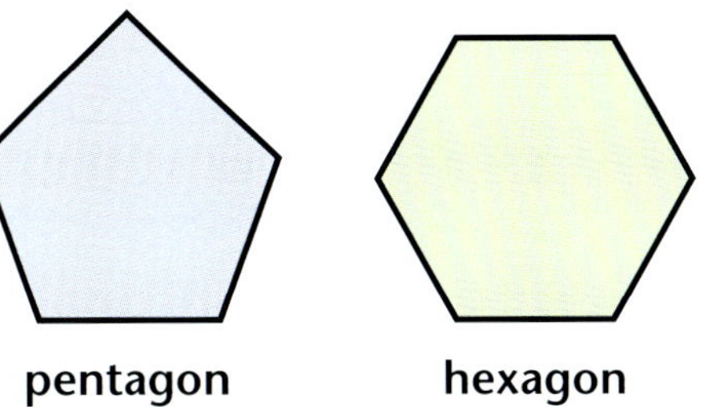

A pentagon is a polygon with 5 sides.
A hexagon is a polygon with 6 sides.

prediction an informed guess about what will happen in the future

prime number a whole number greater than 1 that has only two factors, 1 and itself (*See also* **factors**.)

3, 5, and 7 are examples of prime numbers.

probability a number telling the chance that an event might happen

Three of ten pins are red. The probability of a red pin falling is $\frac{3}{10}$.

pyramid a solid figure whose bottom face is a polygon and whose other faces are triangles with a common vertex (*See also* **face**, **polygon**, **vertex**.)

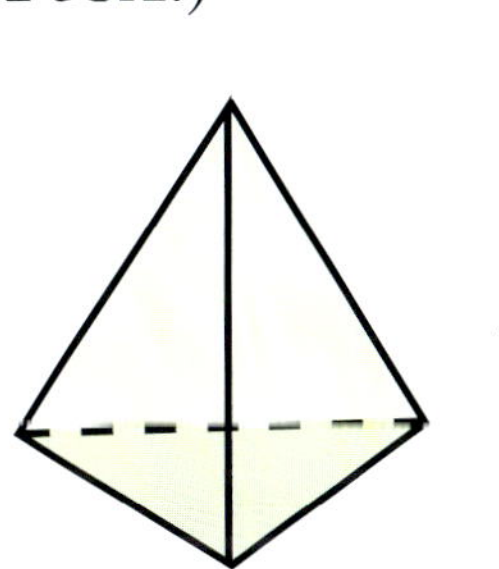

triangle base

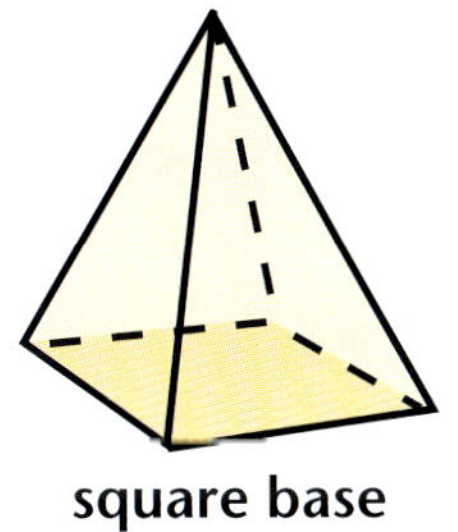

square base

The pyramids in Egypt are thousands of years old.

quadrilateral a polygon with four sides

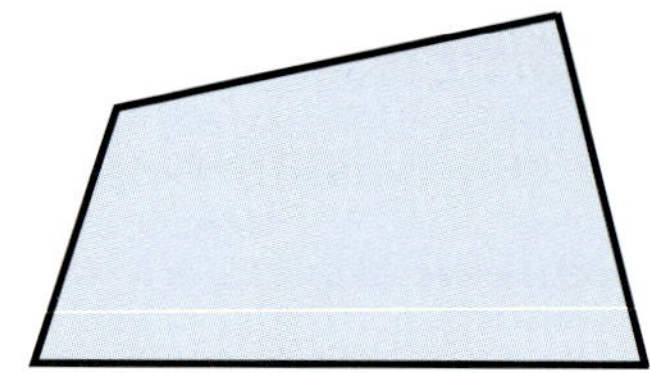

quotient the result of dividing, other than the remainder

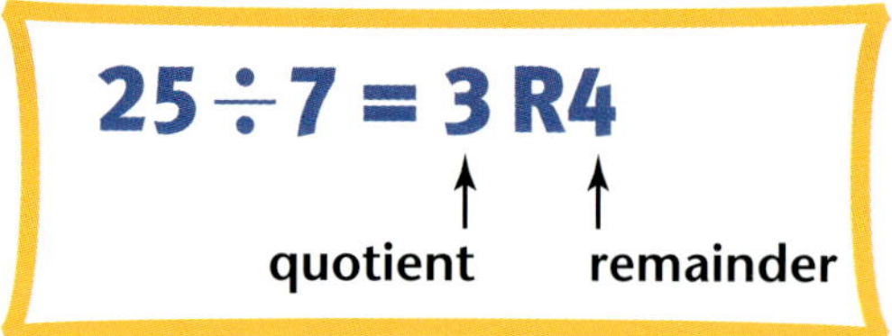

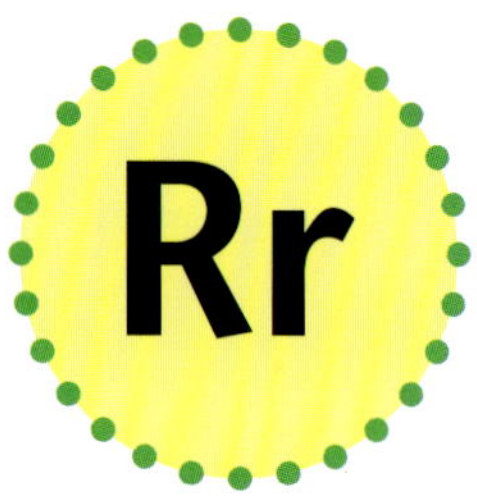

range the difference between the largest number and smallest number in a set of numbers

Test Grades

Student	Grade
Tony	**73**
Tara	77
Lee	82
Mia	**96**

Range **23** (96 – 73 = 23)

ray a part of a line with one endpoint that goes on forever in one direction

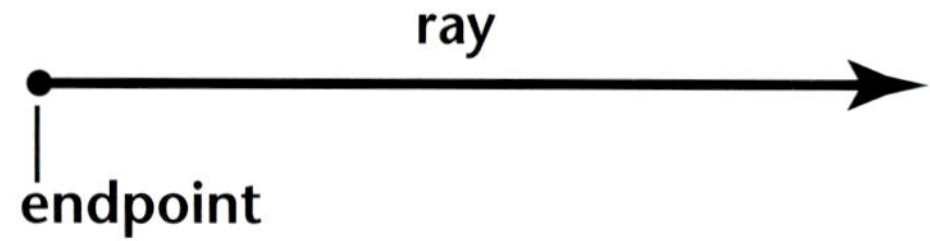

rectangular prism a solid figure with rectangles for all its faces

regroup to use 1 ten to make 10 ones, 1 hundred to form 10 tens, and so on

rhombus a parallelogram with all four sides of the same length (*See also* **parallelogram**.)

right angle an angle that is 90° (*See also* **angle**.)

right angle

rounding changing a number to the nearest ten, hundred, thousand, and so on; when you are rounding to ten, if a number is less than 5, round down—if a number is 5 or greater, round up

45 rounds up to 50 to the nearest ten.
32 rounds down to 30 to the nearest ten.

scalene triangle a triangle with no equal sides and no equal angles (*See also* **angle**.)

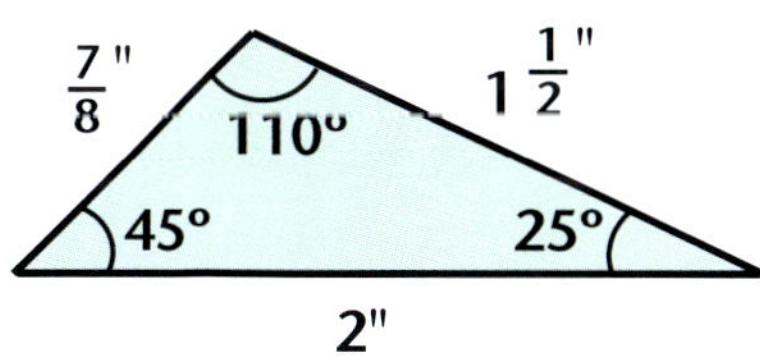

side a line segment of a polygon (*See also* **polygon**.)

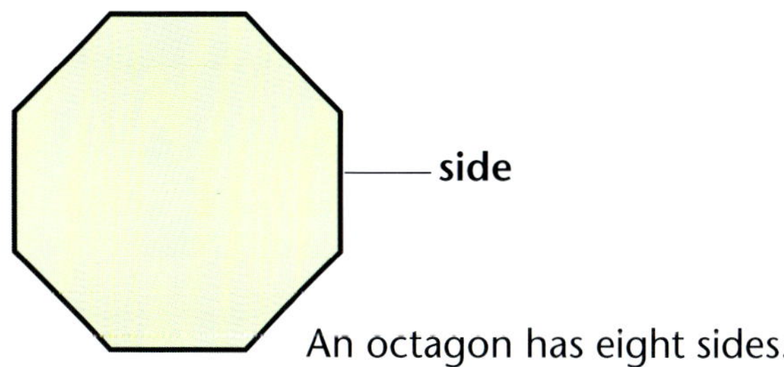

An octagon has eight sides.

similar figures figures with the same shape that may differ in size

These triangles differ in size but have equal angles.

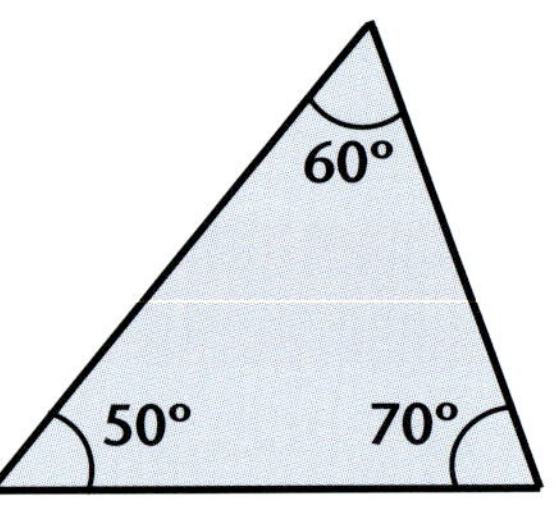

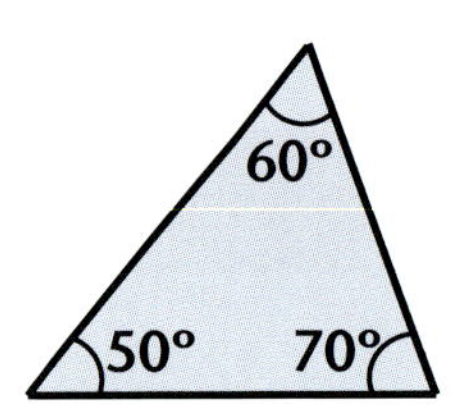

simplest form a fraction in its lowest terms—the numerator and denominator have no common factors other than 1 (*See also* **denominator**, **numerator**.)

$\frac{3}{5}$ is the simplest form of $\frac{6}{10}$

solid figure a figure that has length, width, height, and volume—a solid figure has points in more than one plane

A pyramid, cylinder, cone, cube, and sphere are solid figures.

sphere a solid figure that is shaped like a round ball—a sphere has no flat faces and no edges or vertices

These balls used to play sports are spheres.

square a four-sided polygon with all sides of the same length and four 90° angles (*See also* **angle**, **polygon**.)

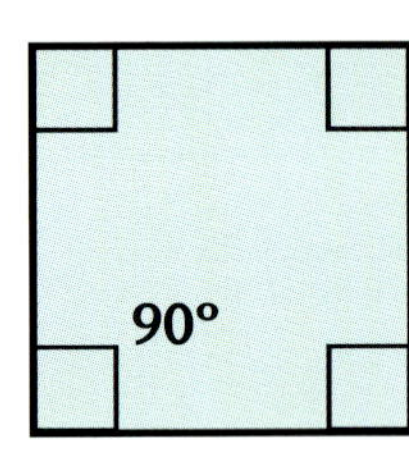

straight angle an angle that forms a straight line; a straight angle is 180°

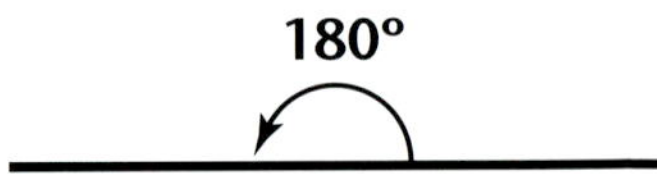

sum the number that results from adding two addends

$34 + 16 = 50$

addends ↑ ↑ sum ↑

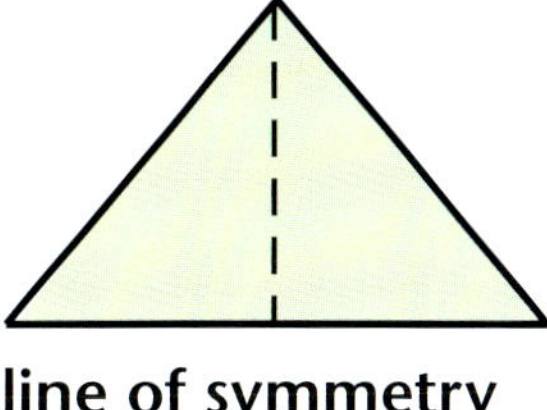

line of symmetry

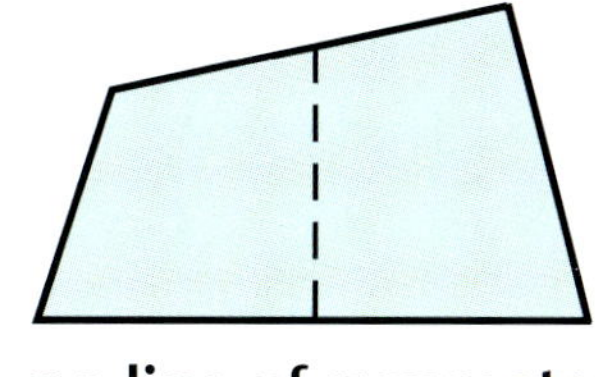

no line of symmetry

symmetry if a figure can be folded so that both parts match exactly, the figure has symmetry

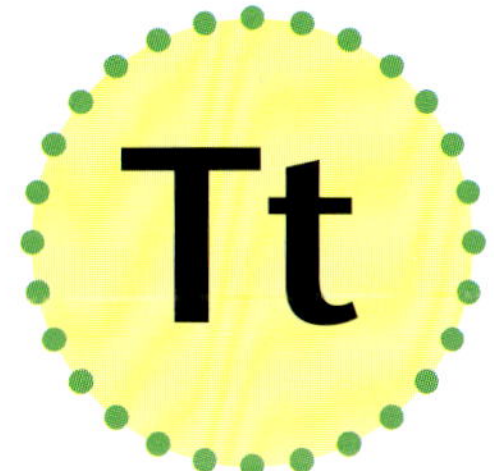

tenth one part of a whole that has ten equal parts

One seedling is one-tenth ($\frac{1}{10}$) of the total number of seedlings.

trapezoid a four-sided polygon with only two parallel sides (*See also* **polygon**, **parallel lines**.)

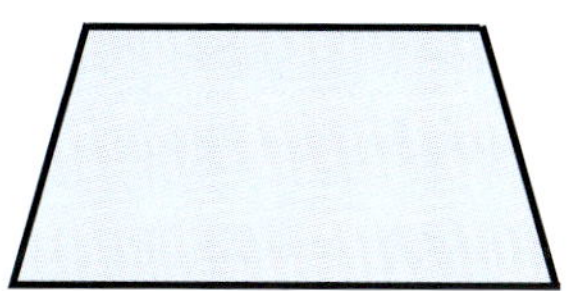

tree diagram a diagram of branches that show the possible outcomes of an event

First Coin Toss	Second Coin Toss	Outcome
Heads	Heads	Heads, Heads
	Tails	Heads, Tails
Tails	Heads	Tails, Heads
	Tails	Tails, Tails

possible outcomes when a coin is tossed twice

triangular prism a long, solid triangle: two faces are triangles, three faces are rectangles (*See also* **face**.)

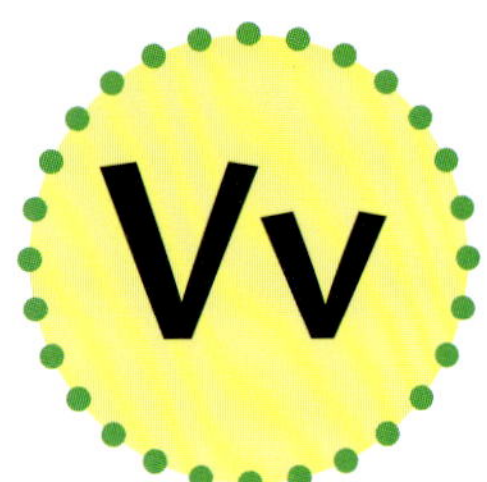

variable a letter standing for a number; variables are used in algebraic expressions

$2y = x$
x and y are variables.
If y is 2, x is 4; if y is 3, x is 6.

vertex (*plural* **vertices**) point where two lines meet to form an angle; where two sides of a polygon meet, or three or more edges of a solid figure meet (*See also* **angle**, **face**, **polygon**.)

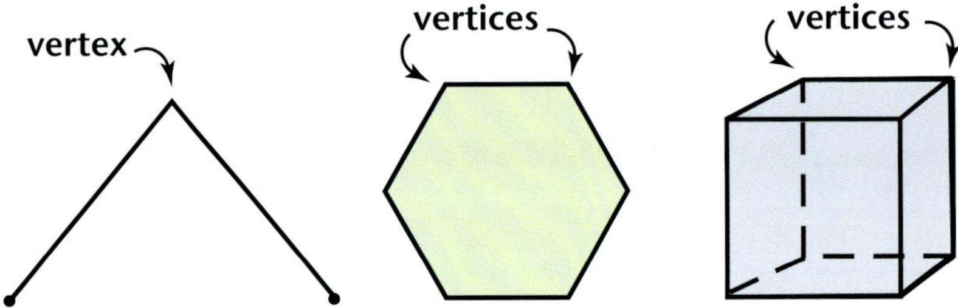

volume amount of space in a solid figure; to find the volume of a rectangular prism, multiply the length times the width times the height, or $V = l \times w \times h$

To find the volume of this box, multiply the length by the width by the height, or $l \times w \times h$.

Zero Property the sum of a number and 0 is that number; the product of a number and 0 is 0

$9 + 0 = 9$
$9 \times 0 = 0$